SEASONAL WEATHER

WINTER
WEATHER

John Mason

Seasonal Weather

Spring Weather
Summer Weather
Autumn Weather
Winter Weather

Cover: A sunset over a bare wintry landscape.

Opposite: Deep snow covering fields in winter.

Edited by Sarah Doughty
Series designed by Derek Lee

First published in 1990 by
Wayland (Publishers) Ltd
61, Western Road, Hove
East Sussex, BN3 1JD, England

British Library Cataloguing in Publication Data
Mason, John
   Winter weather — (seasonal weather)
   1. Weather
   I. Title II. Weather
   551.5
   574.543

   ISBN 1–85210–921–1

Typeset by Nicola Taylor, Wayland
Printed and bound by Casterman S.A., Belgium

CONTENTS

What is winter?

A cold, misty winter's morning with snow on the ground.

When many people think of winter they think of very cold weather, long dark evenings, ice and snow. But some parts of the Earth have no real winter at all. In the **tropics** near the **Equator** many people have never seen ice or snow. Day and night are of nearly equal length all year and the weather is almost always very warm.

At the **poles** it is always bitterly cold. There are long, dark freezing winters when the Sun never shines. The cold landscape is swept by fierce snowstorms. The poles have

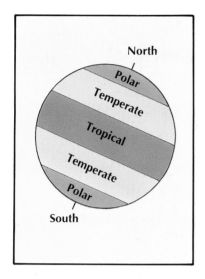

The mild temperate regions lie between the freezing poles and the warm tropical regions.

short, cool summers, when the Sun shines for twenty-four hours a day. Huge areas of land and sea lie under thick snow and ice even in summer.

Between the poles and the tropics are the **temperate regions**, where the length of day and night vary during the year. It stays light until the early evening in summer but gets dark in the late afternoon in winter. Winter is part of a never-ending cycle of seasons – spring, summer, autumn and winter. While the temperate lands of the northern **hemisphere** freeze in winter, the southern hemisphere enjoys warm summer weather.

Children dressed for winter in warm coats and hats.

Why seasons happen

During the year, the Earth moves around the Sun. The Earth also spins on its **axis**. This axis, which passes through the North and South Poles, is not upright, but leans over at an angle of 23.5˚. This tilt causes the seasons. If one hemisphere is tilted towards the Sun, the other is tilted away. When the northern hemisphere is tilted away from the Sun, it is winter in the north. Meanwhile the south enjoys its summer.

▲ **In temperate regions in winter the Sun is low in the sky.**

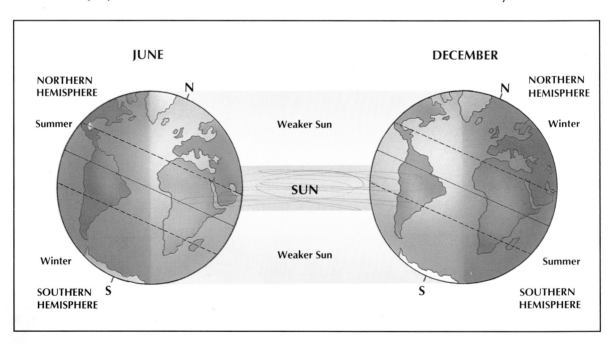

JUNE
DECEMBER

NORTHERN HEMISPHERE
N
NORTHERN HEMISPHERE
N

Summer
Weaker Sun
Winter

SUN

Winter
Weaker Sun
Summer

SOUTHERN HEMISPHERE
S
S
SOUTHERN HEMISPHERE

When each hemisphere in turn is tilted away from the Sun, it is winter in that half of the world and summer in the other.

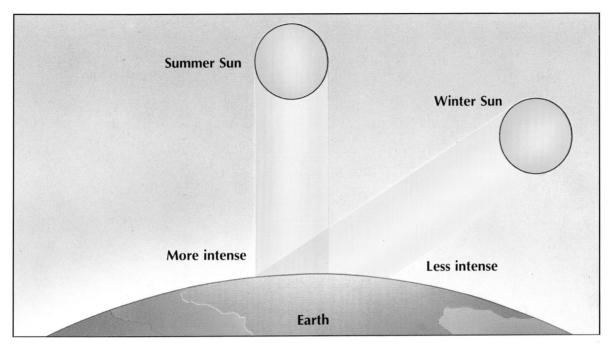

The Sun's position in winter makes it colder than summer.

Six months later, the northern hemisphere is tilted towards the Sun and it is summer there.

In winter, the Sun is much lower in the sky than it is in summer. It spends less time above the **horizon**, so the days are shorter and the nights longer. The Sun's rays also strike the ground at a shallower angle. They are spread over a wider area, so their heating effect is less. When the Sun is low down its rays must pass through more atmosphere to reach the Earth, which further weakens them. The weakness of the Sun's rays and the shorter days make winter colder than summer.

Northern Hemisphere			
Autumn	Winter	Spring	Summer
September	December	March	June
October	January	April	July
November	February	May	August
Spring	Summer	Autumn	Winter
Southern Hemisphere			

Winter weather

Snow lies deep on the ground in Norway in winter.

As the southern hemisphere tilts towards the Sun, days become shorter in the northern temperate regions. The shortest day falls on 21 December. This is known as the Winter Solstice (or Midwinter Day) and comes near the beginning of winter, not in the middle. As the days grow shorter, the air, land and oceans retain some heat from the summer sunshine. Only when they have cooled completely, does the really cold winter weather begin. This is not until late January or February.

In the southern temperate regions, winter occurs in June, July and August, with late July and August being the coldest period. As in the north, the coldest weather occurs long after the Winter Solstice on 21 June.

When cold winter winds blow, the temperature may drop to many degrees below freezing point (0°C or 32°F). Heavy snow falls in Canada, the northern USA, Scandinavia, Siberia and in the mountains of the European Alps and the Highlands of Scotland.

Frost often occurs in winter and sometimes pieces of ice fall, known as hailstones. During the long winter nights fog and mist may form over open countryside or in valleys. They may persist during the day because the Sun's rays are too weak to drive them away.

Hailstones are pieces of ice that fall to the ground. They may measure over 10 mm across.

The Sun's winter rays are too weak to drive away morning fog.

When the wind blows

Cool winds blow over India from the Himalayas in winter.

The winds which blow in every part of the Earth result from differences in **air pressure**. As air is heated, it expands becoming lighter. It then rises, leaving an area of low pressure. Cooler air moves in to replace it. As cool air is heavier, it sinks producing a region of high air pressure. The flow of cold air from a high pressure area into a neighbouring region of low pressure causes a wind to blow.

The air at the poles is always being cooled. It sinks, creating a high pressure area. Near the Equator, where the air is warm is a band of low pressure. This air rises and flows north and south. It cools and sinks at **latitudes** 30° north and 30° south creating two bands of high pressure. Because winds always blow from high to low pressure, winds called Trade Winds blow towards the Equator and **Westerlies** blow towards temperate latitudes.

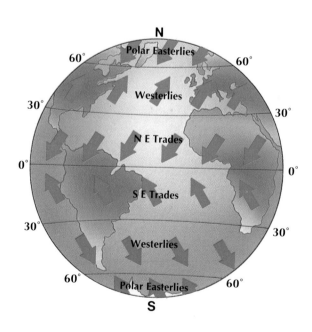

A diagram showing the main surface winds on Earth.

As cool air from the poles flows towards the temperate regions it is warmed, and rises at latitudes 60° north and 60° south creating two bands of low pressure. It is here that the warm Westerlies meet the colder **Polar Easterlies**.

Some winds are seasonal, such as winter **monsoons**. Indian summers are hot, but in winter the land cools quickly. The air above the Indian plains sinks, forming a region of high pressure. A dry monsoon wind then blows from the north-west overland, becoming north-easterly. It blows towards the Indian Ocean which is a warmer area of low pressure.

Easterly winds blow over South-east Asia. Winter winds also blow from the north-west over northern China and from the north-east over south-east China.

In winter, regions of low pressure across central Asia and northern China cause strong, bitterly cold winds to blow from Siberia in the north, bringing fierce snowstorms to Russia, Mongolia and Manchuria.

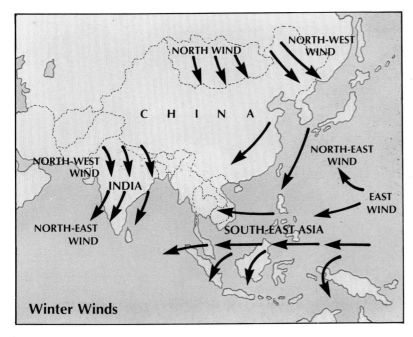

Winter Winds

In winter, monsoon winds blow over India, China and South-east Asia.

Clouds and water vapour

As the Sun's rays heat the surface of the oceans, liquid water is changed into water vapour by **evaporation**. Water vapour is an invisible gas which mixes with other gases that make up the air we breathe. It is water vapour which produces the clouds that give us rain, hail and snow.

When air is warmed over land or sea it absorbs water vapour. This moist air then rises, but as it does so it cools. When air is cooled below its **dewpoint**, some of the water vapour turns back into tiny droplets of water. This is called condensation. These water droplets collect together to become visible as clouds.

Clouds forming over oceans are blown by winds until they meet the coastal slopes of mountains on land. Forced upwards by air currents, they cool and heavy rain falls. Across the mountains, in the **rain shadow**, the clouds descend to drier air. The water drops turn back into vapour and the rain stops.

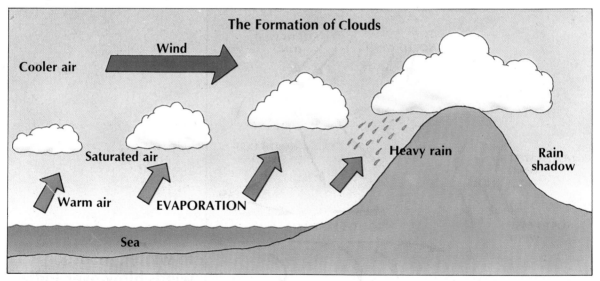

The Formation of Clouds

Cooler air — Wind — Saturated air — Warm air — EVAPORATION — Heavy rain — Rain shadow — Sea

Clouds that form over oceans rise and cool over coastal slopes of mountains and heavy rain falls.

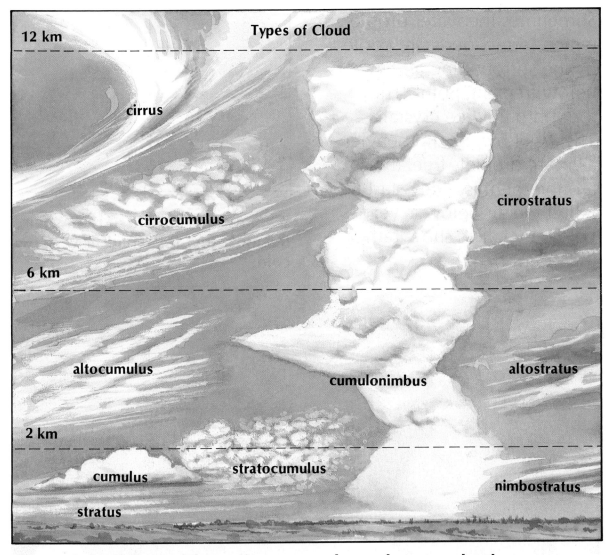

Types of Cloud

12 km

cirrus

cirrocumulus

cirrostratus

6 km

altocumulus

cumulonimbus

altostratus

2 km

cumulus

stratocumulus

nimbostratus

stratus

Types of cloud formed from cirrus, cumulus and stratus clouds.

There are three main types of clouds – stratus, cumulus and cirrus, but these can combine to produce other types. Stratus clouds look like grey blankets stretching across the sky. Cumulus clouds may appear like lumps of fluffy wool or billow out like huge cauliflowers. Cirrus clouds are thin, feathery curling wisps, very high up in the sky.

Snow, fog and frosts

Sometimes the water droplets which form clouds are cooled by the surrounding air to below freezing point. They form into tiny ice crystals. These get bigger and heavier as more droplets freeze around them, so they start to fall. If the air below is very cold they fall as snow rather than rain.

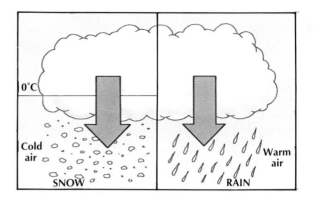

▲ **Snow falls instead of rain when the air below the clouds is very cold.**

Snow and hoar frost in winter in the state of Colorado, USA.

Mountain fog forms in Alpine valleys in Switzerland in winter.

Ice forms when water freezes. Ice is lighter than water and can often be seen floating on lakes and rivers.

On clear, cold winter nights, the land cools quickly. As the warm, moist air in contact with the ground cools to below the dewpoint, its water vapour condenses into millions of tiny water droplets suspended in the air. This is mist or fog. It can also form at sea when a warm **ocean current** meets colder water.

Sometimes on cold winter nights, water vapour condenses from the air on to the ground as crystals of ice when the dewpoint is below freezing. This is called hoar frost and covers the ground, trees and fences with a thin white layer.

Cold polar lands

At the North Pole, in the Arctic, huge sheets of ice and snow cover the ocean. They extend into Greenland and northern parts of Canada and Europe. At the South Pole, the Antarctic land mass is also covered by a thick layer of ice. These are called **ice-caps**.

Near the poles, winter is the longest season lasting for eight or nine months. During winter in polar regions, the air is so very cold that any water which falls from the clouds quickly freezes into ice crystals and falls as snow.

Winter begins in August or September in the Arctic. The edge of the sea begins to freeze as the Sun sinks lower in the sky. At the North Pole, the Sun sets in late September and does not rise again until

Inuit children on Baffin Island, Canada, in the Arctic.

An iceberg in the South Orkneys near Antarctica. Here the Sun rises in midwinter but remains very low in the sky.

late March. Without sunshine, the Arctic seas grow cold, and moist ocean winds bring winter storms and heavy snow in January to parts of the Arctic.

The worst winters on Earth are those that grip the South Pole. The Antarctic winds blow very strongly. Cold, heavy air pours off the ice-cap and gales roar across the continent, whipping up snow from the ground into fierce snowstorms or blizzards.

Cold Polar Lands

The coldest area in the world is in the Antarctic.

At Vostok, 1,300 km from the South Pole, the July temperature has sunk as low as -89.2°C (-128.6°F).

Winter around the world

In winter, the land cools more rapidly than the sea. This means that continents in the northern temperate regions are coldest in January, but the oceans are coldest in March. Places near the sea have mild winters and are coldest late in the season. In mid-continent, winters are more severe and lowest temperatures occur earlier.

Winter in the temperate regions is less harsh than winter at the poles. Westward-facing coasts have rain and snow, but the frosts are less severe than in mid-continent. Sometimes, winter weather is affected by warm winds blowing from the tropics or icy winds from the poles. In north-western Europe, there is a continual conflict between mild air blowing from the south-west over the Atlantic Ocean, and bitterly cold Siberian air from the east.

In Canada, the USA and USSR, cold Arctic winds

▲ Winter snowfall covers the rocks in Bryce Canyon National Park, Utah, USA.

Skiing is popular around the world. These skiers are in Victoria, Australia.

stream down from the North Pole because there are no mountain ranges to act as barriers. In the southern hemisphere, cold Antarctic winds sweep northwards, bringing severe weather to Australia, Patagonia in South America and even Southern Africa. In the USA, warm air flows up the Mississippi valley from the Gulf of Mexico, but when it meets cold air from the Arctic it causes snow-storms in the central states.

▲ **Bitterly cold winters are common in the USSR where snow covers Red Square.**

Stockholm, Sweden has snow in winter, but does not get as cold as the neighbouring USSR due to mild south-west winds.

Very cold winters

Snow falls over every continent in the world, but at low latitudes it only falls on the tops of high mountains. In the tropics, snowfalls are extremely rare. It snowed in and around Riyadh in Saudi Arabia on 1 January 1973, clinging to trees but not settling. Snow also fell in the Kalahari Desert in southern Africa on 1 September 1981 for the first time in living memory.

In temperate regions, snow falls regularly in winter. It lies on the ground wherever the air temperature is below 3°C (37°F) and stays on the ground all season if the temperature of the coldest month is below -3°C (27°F). The lowest temperatures occur when cold winds blow and there is heavy cloud that blocks the Sun during the day. Inland areas suffer colder winters than places nearer the sea. So in

Lowest Recorded Temperatures	
ANTARCTICA Vostok	**-89°C/-128°F**
ASIA Oimyakon, Siberia	**-68°C/-90°F**
NORTH AMERICA Snag, Yukon	**-63°C/-81°F**
AFRICA Ilfrane, Morocco	**-24°C/-11°F**
AUSTRALASIA Charlotte Pass New South Wales	**-22°C/-8°F**
EUROPE Ust'Schchugor USSR	**-55°C/-67°F**

Snow in the Arizona Desert, USA only falls in very harsh winters.

London, the average lowest January temperature is 1.7°C (34.5°F) but in Moscow it is -13°C (8.6°F).

The world's greatest snowfalls have all happened in the USA. The Rocky Mountains have an average annual snowfall of 7.6–10 m. The snowiest winter in the eastern and midwestern states was in 1977–8 when it began snowing in October.

▲ **In Winnipeg, Canada, the freezing weather has caused roads to be blocked.**

In the exceptionally cold winter of 1963, the sea froze in Herne Bay, Kent in Britain.

The importance of the oceans

Fiords in Norway are kept ice-free during winter by the warm waters of the Gulf Stream.

You might expect that the closer to the poles you go, the colder the climate becomes. This is usually true, but ocean currents play a major role in controlling the climate of certain places on Earth. These currents are movements of water driven by wind and deflected by the shape of the land. Currents flow to different regions of the world and affect the normal temperatures there.

Parts of north-western Europe have a very mild winter climate. They are affected by the warm waters of an ocean current called the Gulf Stream. This brings warm water from the Gulf of Mexico north-eastwards across the

Atlantic Ocean to Europe. Passing around the British Isles, it continues northwards along the coast of Norway and enters the **Arctic Circle**.

By contrast, Newfoundland, which is further south, lies within the cold waters of the Labrador current. This sweeps southwards from the Arctic Ocean along the eastern coast of Canada. So while the fiords of Norway remain free from ice in winter, the Saint Lawrence River in Canada is covered with thick ice, although it lies 2,400 km further south.

The snowbound Saint Lawrence River, Canada, in winter.

Ice ages and climatic change

For the past million years or so, the Earth's climate has alternated between warmer and cooler periods. In the cold periods, called ice ages, the polar ice sheets grow much larger to cover surrounding continents. We also know that between 120,000 and 75,000 years ago, the Earth's climate was fairly warm, a period known as an interglacial.

The Tasman Glacier near South Canterbury, New Zealand.

The last ice age began about 65,000 years ago and led to heavy ice coverage until about 25,000 years ago. Much of Europe was covered by **glaciers** and deep snow until about 10,000 years ago, but since then the climate has been warmer.

Short-term changes have occurred more recently. The period between 1550 and 1850 has been called the Little Ice Age. During that time, glaciers moved further than at any time since the last ice age. The Arctic pack ice also moved further south. During the cold winters at this time, frost fairs were held in London on the River Thames which had frozen over.

A painting of the last known frost fair in London in 1814.

Forecasting winter weather

Weather forecasters collect data on weather conditions. **Satellites**, ships, aircraft, weather balloons and local weather stations provide information about the weather. Details of air pressure, temperature, rainfall, winds and sunshine are then fed into a large computer. The computer analyses the data so accurate forecasts can be made for the days ahead.

Air moves from places where its pressure is high to regions of lower air pressure. Areas of low pressure, called depressions, are usually circular in shape on weather maps. Depressions often mean disturbed, windy weather. High pressure regions, or anticyclones, bring lighter winds and generally more settled weather. These still conditions can cause frost and fog in winter. The weather can also be affected by large masses of warm or cold air.

When two of these **air masses** meet, the border between them is called a front. Clouds form along the front, which produce rain and sometimes snow in winter.

A weather balloon being launched from a weather station in Colorado, USA.

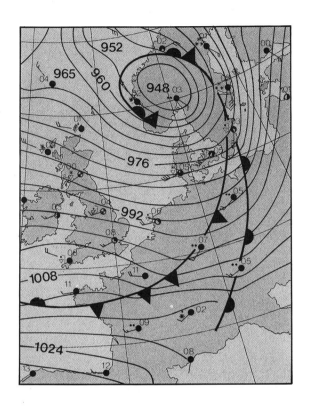

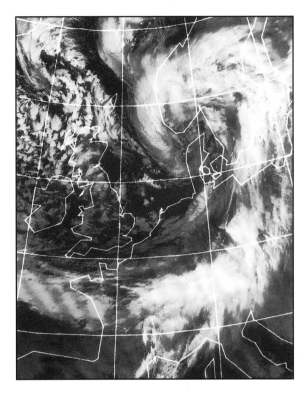

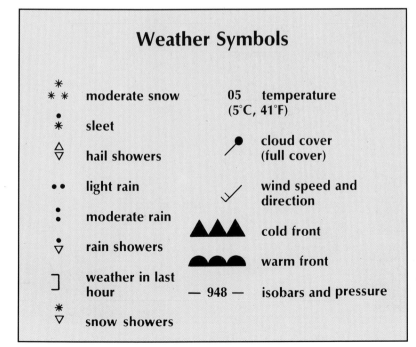

Weather Symbols

✳✳ **moderate snow**
✳•

•
✳ **sleet**

△
▽ **hail showers**

•• **light rain**

• **moderate rain**

•
▽ **rain showers**

⌐ **weather in last
hour**

✳
▽ **snow showers**

05 **temperature
(5°C, 41°F)**

● **cloud cover
(full cover)**

✓ **wind speed and
direction**

▲▲▲ **cold front**

●●● **warm front**

— 948 — **isobars and pressure**

A weather map and a satellite picture taken on a winter's day in northern Europe, showing a deep depression with heavy cloud along both fronts. The weather is wet and stormy. The key explains what the weather symbols mean.

Things to do – measuring temperature

An interesting project for winter is to keep a daily record of the highest and lowest air temperatures. The easiest way to do this is to use thermometers. A thermometer contains a liquid which expands and rises up a thin glass tube against a scale as the temperature rises. On cooling the liquid contracts and drops back down the tube.

Greatest Temperature Variations

The greatest seasonal variations in temperature occur in the centre of large continental land masses.

At Verkhoyansk in north-eastern Siberia a lowest winter temperature of -68°C (-90.4°F) has been recorded, and a highest summer temperature of 36.7°C (98°F). This is a range of 104.7°C (188.4°F).

Taking a reading of the thermometers in a Stevenson screen.

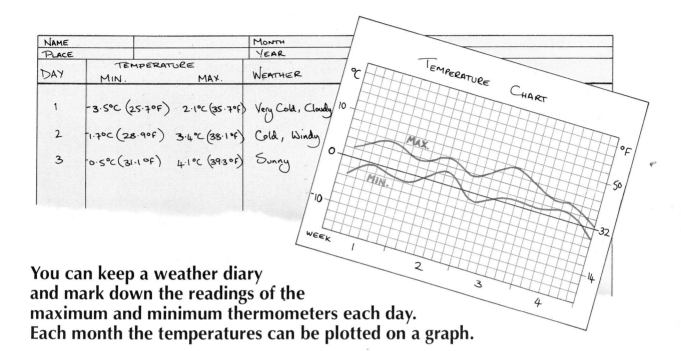

NAME			MONTH	
PLACE			YEAR	
DAY	TEMPERATURE		WEATHER	
	MIN.	MAX.		
1	-3.5°C (25.7°F)	2.1°C (35.7°F)	Very Cold, Cloudy	
2	-1.7°C (28.9°F)	3.4°C (38.1°F)	Cold, Windy	
3	-0.5°C (31.1°F)	4.1°C (39.3°F)	Sunny	

**You can keep a weather diary
and mark down the readings of the
maximum and minimum thermometers each day.
Each month the temperatures can be plotted on a graph.**

A maximum thermometer records the highest air temperatures. It is a glass tube with a narrow waist near the bulb which contains mercury. Once the mercury level has risen to the highest temperature, the waist prevents it flowing back into the bulb. Shaking returns the mercury to the bulb.

A minimum thermometer uses alcohol because it has a very low freezing point. It contains a marker that is able to slide within the liquid. As the alcohol level falls, the marker is dragged down the tube, but is left marking the lowest temperature when the level rises again.

For an accurate reading it is important to place the thermometers correctly. They should be out of direct sunshine and not too near the ground. At a weather station they would be kept in special outdoor housing called a Stevenson screen. Your own air thermometers could be kept on a shaded, outside wall of your school, about 1.2 m above the ground.

GLOSSARY

Air masses Large areas of warm or cold air in the atmosphere.

Air pressure The force of layers of air in the atmosphere on the layers below, and on the ground.

Arctic Circle An imaginary line around the north polar region.

Axis An imaginary north-south line about which the Earth spins once every day.

Dewpoint The temperature at which water vapour in the air starts to condense into water droplets.

Equator A line that encircles the Earth midway between the North and South Poles.

Evaporation The process by which liquid water becomes a vapour or gas due to heating.

Glacier A slow-moving mass of ice and snow.

Hemisphere Half of the Earth's sphere.

Horizon The line at which the earth and sky appear to meet.

Ice-cap A thick layer of ice covering a large area of land.

Latitude A measure of how far north or south of the Equator a place lies.

Monsoon A wind that changes direction with the seasons.

Ocean current A moving flow of water in the oceans.

Polar Easterlies Easterly winds which blow from the polar regions into the temperate regions.

Poles The extreme north and south of the Earth.

Rain shadow The side of a mountain on which little rain falls.

Satellite A device that circles high above the Earth. Some satellites are used to monitor the Earth's weather.

Temperate regions The areas between the tropics and the poles that have a mild climate.

Tropics A band on the Earth's surface stretching between 25° north and 25° south of the Equator.

Westerlies Westerly winds which blow usually from the direction of the tropics into temperate regions.

BOOKS TO READ

Bramwell, Martyn, **Glaciers and Ice-caps** (Franklin Watts, 1986)
Mabey, Richard, **Cold Comforts** (Hutchinson, 1983)
McInnes, Celia, **Projects for Winter** (Wayland, 1988)
Rosen, Mike, **Winter Festivals** (Wayland, 1990)
Sauvain, Philip, **Snow and Ice** (Franklin Watts, 1978)
Toulson, Shirley, **The Winter Solstice** (Jill Norman & Hobhouse, 1981)
Whitlock, Ralph, **Winter** (Wayland, 1987)

PICTURE ACKNOWLEDGEMENTS

The publishers would like to thank the following for allowing their pictures to be reproduced in this book: Bryan and Cherry Alexander 16, 21 (top); David Bowden Photo Library 18 (bottom); Cephas Picture Library 18 (top); Bruce Coleman Ltd 4, 20; Dundee Meterological Office 27; ET Archive 25; Chris Fairclough Colour Library 6, 19 (both); Geoscience Features 8, 15, 21 (bottom), 22; Eric and David Hosking 9 (top); The Hutchison Library 5; Oxford Scientific Films 17; Tony Stone Worldwide 14, 23, 24, Wayland Picture Library 10 (Jimmy Holmes), 28 (Paul Seheult); Zefa Picture Library cover, inside cover, 9 (bottom), 26. All illustrations by Peter Bull Art except Hayward Art Group 27, 29.

INDEX

Numbers in **bold** refer to illustrations